NEW ENGLAND COOKING

GALLERY BOOKS
An Imprint of W. H. Smith Publishers Inc.
112 Madison Avenue
New York City 10016

Introduction

The recipes of New England are some of the oldest and most traditional in the country. Food played an enormous part in the founding of the United States, which began in this part of the country with the landing of the Pilgrims. During their first year they saw their crops, planted from seed brought with them from home, fail to take hold in the new soil and climate. They had to adapt to survive, and that meant relying on native foods, however strange these seemed. The Indians introduced the Pilgrims to maize, pumpkins, squash, cranberries and their own domesticated turkeys. The Pilgrims were soon using these North American ingredients in many of their favorite recipes from home. These foods that saved the settlers' lives also became part of the Thanksgiving menu that is still enjoyed today. Fish and seafood were important resources from the start and have remained so. But New England has contributed many other good things to American cooking – maple syrup, blueberries for pies, clams for chowder, to name just a few. As immigrants from other countries came to join that first band of settlers, they brought their own influences to bear on a cuisine that retains its traditional connections while being at the same time truly American.

SERVES 6-8

Clam Chowder

French fishermen invented this thick soup-stew, but New Englanders adopted it as their own, using the delicious varieties of clams found along their coastlines.

2lbs clams (1lb shelled or canned clams)
3oz rindless bacon, diced
2 medium onions, finely diced
1 tbsp flour
6 medium potatoes, peeled and cubed
Salt and pepper
4 cups milk
1 cup light cream
Chopped parsley (optional)

Step 1 Cook the clams until the shells open. Stir occasionally for even cooking.

1. Scrub the clams well and place them in a basin of cold water with a handful of flour to soak for 30 minutes. Drain the clams and place them in a deep saucepan with about ½ cup cold water. Cover and bring to the boil, stirring occasionally until all the shells open. Discard any shells that do not open. Strain the clam liquid and reserve it and set the clams aside to cool.

2. Place the diced bacon in a large, deep saucepan and cook slowly until the fat is rendered. Turn up the heat and brown the bacon. Remove it to paper towel to drain.

Step 2 Cook the bacon slowly until the fat renders.

Step 3 Cook the onion in the bacon fat until soft and transluscent.

3. Add the onion to the bacon fat in the pan and cook slowly to soften. Stir in the flour and add the potatoes, salt, pepper, milk and reserved clam juice.

4. Cover and bring to the boil and cook for about 10 minutes, or until the potatoes are nearly tender. Remove the clams from their shells and chop them if large. Add to the soup along with the cream and diced bacon. Cook a further 10 minutes, or until the potatoes and clams are tender. Add the chopped parsley, if desired, and serve immediately.

Cook's Notes

Time
Preparation takes about 30 minutes and cooking takes about 20 minutes.

Cook's Tip
Soaking clams and other shellfish in water with flour or cornmeal before cooking plumps them up and also helps to eliminate sand and grit.

Buying Guide
If fresh or canned clams are not available, substitute mussels or cockles instead.

SERVES 8-10

A GREEN-PEAS SOUP

This is a summery version of a hearty winter staple. Green peas and mint add a freshness and a light, delicate taste to dried split peas.

¾ cup dried split peas
1¼lbs frozen peas
3oz fresh mint leaves
½ cup butter or margarine, melted
Pinch salt and pepper
Sprigs of fresh mint to garnish

Step 1 Cook the split peas in water until very soft. Test by mashing some against the side of the pan.

1. Place the split peas with about 6 cups water in a heavy saucepan. Cover, bring to the boil and cook until very tender, about 40 minutes.

2. Strain the peas and reserve the liquid.

3. Pour the liquid back into the saucepan and add the frozen peas. Chop the mint leaves, reserving some for garnish, and add to the peas. Bring to the boil in a covered saucepan.

Step 3 Cook the frozen peas in the reserved split pea liquid along with the chopped mint.

Step 4 Puree the split peas and stir them back into the soup, mixing well.

4. Meanwhile, add the melted butter to the dried peas and push through a strainer or work in a food processor to form a smooth purée. Add the purée to the green peas, mixing well. Add salt and pepper to taste.

5. Pour the hot soup into a tureen and garnish with sprigs or leaves of mint. Serve immediately.

Cook's Notes

Time
Preparation takes about 30 minutes, cooking takes 45-50 minutes.

Variation
Other fresh herbs, such as marjoram, chervil or thyme may be substituted for the mint.

Buying Guide
Dried split peas are readily available in supermarkets and health food stores.

SERVES 4

Fresh Creamed Mushrooms

For a recipe that has been around since Colonial times, this one is surprisingly up-to-date.

1lb even-sized button mushrooms
1 tbsp lemon juice
2 tbsps butter or margarine
1 tbsp flour
Salt and white pepper
¼ tsp freshly grated nutmeg
1 small bay leaf
1 blade mace
1 cup heavy cream
1 tbsp dry sherry

Step 1 Trim the mushroom stems level with the caps. Do not use the stems for this recipe.

1. Wash the mushrooms quickly and dry them well. Trim the stems level with the caps. Leave whole if small, halve or quarter if large. Toss with the lemon juice and set aside.

2. In a medium saucepan, melt the butter or margarine and stir in the flour. Cook, stirring gently, for about 1 minute. Remove from the heat, add the nutmeg, salt, pepper, bay leaf and mace and gradually stir in the cream.

Step 2 Cook the flour gently in the butter for about 1 minute.

Step 3 Test with a sharp knife to see if the mushrooms are tender.

3. Return the pan to the heat and bring to the boil, stirring constantly. Allow to boil for about 1 minute, or until thickened. Reduce the heat and add the mushrooms. Simmer gently, covered, for about 5 minutes, or until the mushrooms are tender. Add the sherry during the last few minutes of cooking. Remove bay leaf and blade mace. Sprinkle with additional grated nutmeg before serving.

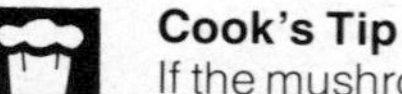

Cook's Tip
If the mushrooms are clean, do not wash them. If washing is necessary, rinse them very quickly and pat dry quickly. Mushrooms absorb water easily.

Time
Preparation takes about 20 minutes, and cooking takes about 7 minutes.

Variation
The recipe may be used as a sauce for chicken or ham as well.

Serving Ideas
Serve on hot toast or in individual custard cups or scallop shells, accompanied with hot buttered toast or melba toast. Serves 4 as an appetizer.

SERVES 6-8

Cream of Pumpkin Soup

Pumpkins have an honoured place in American culinary history and show up in many different preparations. Their excellent colour and texture make a distinctive soup.

1 large pumpkin about 4-5lbs in weight
¼ cup butter or margarine
1 large onion, sliced
1 cup heavy cream
Pinch salt, white pepper and nutmeg
Snipped chives to garnish

1. Wash the pumpkin well on the outside and cut through horizontally, about 2 inches down from the stem end.

2. Carefully cut most of the pulp off the top and reserve the "lid" for later use.

3. Remove the seeds from the inside and discard them.

4. Using a small, sharp knife, carefully remove all but ½ inch of the pulp from inside the pumpkin. Work slowly and carefully to avoid piercing the outer skin of the pumpkin. Chop all the pulp from the top of the pumpkin and the inside and set it aside.

5. Melt the butter or margarine in a large saucepan and add the onion. Cook slowly until the onion is tender but not brown. Add the pumpkin flesh and about 4 cups cold water. Bring to the boil and then allow to simmer gently, covered, for about 20 minutes.

6. Purée the mixture in a food processor or blender in several small batches. Return the soup to the pot and add the cream, salt, pepper and nutmeg to taste. Reheat the soup and pour it into the reserved pumpkin shell. Garnish the top of the soup with snipped chives, if desired, before serving.

Step 2 Using a large, sharp knife, cut the top off the pumpkin to serve as a lid.

Step 3 Remove the seeds and stringy pulp from inside the pumpkin and discard.

Step 4 Using a small, sharp knife, work slowly to remove the pulp from inside the pumpkin. Leave a layer of flesh on the skin to form a shell.

Cook's Notes

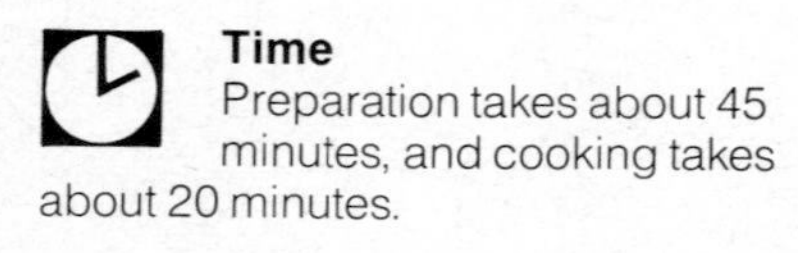

Time
Preparation takes about 45 minutes, and cooking takes about 20 minutes.

Preparation
If desired, 2 pumpkins may be used, 1 for making the soup and 1 to serve as a tureen. The pumpkin used for cooking must be peeled first.

Variation
Canned pumpkin may also be used for the soup instead of fresh. Soup may be served in a tureen or individual bowls instead of the pumpkin shell, if desired.

SERVES 4

Cape Cod Mussels

When seafood is as good as that from Cape Cod, even the simplest preparations stand out.

4½lbs mussels in their shells
Flour or cornmeal
1 cup dry white wine
1 large onion, finely chopped
2-4 cloves garlic, finely chopped
Salt and coarsely ground black pepper
2 bay leaves
1 cup butter, melted
Juice of 1 lemon

1. Scrub the mussels well and remove any barnacles and beards (seaweed strands). Use a stiff brush to scrub the shells, and discard any mussels with broken shells or those that do not close when tapped.

2. Place the mussels in a basin full of cold water with a handful of flour or cornmeal and leave to soak for 30 minutes.

3. Drain the mussels and place them in a large, deep saucepan with the remaining ingredients, except the butter and lemon juice. Cover the pan and bring to the boil.

4. Stir the mussels occasionally while they are cooking to help them cook evenly. Cook about 5-8 minutes, or until the shells open. Discard any mussels that do not open.

5. Spoon the mussels into individual serving bowls and strain the cooking liquid. Pour the liquid into 4 small bowls and serve with the mussels and a bowl of melted butter mixed with lemon juice for each person. Dip the mussels into the broth and the melted butter to eat. Use a mussel shell to scoop out each mussel, or eat with small forks or spoons.

Step 1 Scrub the mussels with a stiff brush to remove barnacles and seaweed beards.

Step 1 To test if the mussels are still alive, tap them on a work surface – the shells should close.

Step 5 Hold a mussel shell between 2 fingers and pinch together to remove mussels from their shells to eat.

Cook's Notes

Time
Preparation takes about 30 minutes, and cooking takes about 5-8 minutes.

Cook's Tip
The beards are strands of seaweed that anchor the mussels to the rocks on which they grow. These must be removed before cooking. They can be pulled off quite easily by hand, or scrubbed off with a stiff brush.

Variation
The same recipe may be prepared with clams. Use the amount of garlic that suits your own taste or leave out the garlic, if desired. Chopped fresh herbs may be added.

SERVES 6

HARVARD BEETS

One of the best known dishes using this readily available root vegetable. The color makes this a perfect accompaniment to plain meat or poultry.

2lbs small beets
Boiling water
3 tbsps cornstarch
½ cup sugar
Pinch salt and pepper
1 cup white wine vinegar
¾ cup reserved beet cooking liquid
2 tbsps butter

Step 3 The peel should pull easily off the beets with a sharp knife.

1. Choose even-sized beets and cut off the tops, if necessary. Place beets in a large saucepan of water. Cover the pan and bring to the boil. Lower the heat and cook gently until tender, about 30-40 minutes. Add more boiling water as necessary during cooking.

2. Drain the beets, reserving the liquid, and allow the beets to cool.

Step 3 Slice the beets into thin rounds.

Step 4 Combine all the sauce ingredients and cook until the cornstarch thickens and clears.

3. When the beets are cool, peel them and slice into ¼ inch rounds, or cut into small dice.

4. Combine the cornstarch, sugar, salt and pepper, vinegar and required amount of beet liquid in a large saucepan. Bring to the boil over moderate heat, stirring constantly until thickened. Return the beets to the saucepan and allow to heat through for about 5 minutes. Stir in the butter and serve immediately.

Cook's Notes

Time
Preparation takes about 20 minutes, and cooking takes about 30-40 minutes for the beets, 5 minutes for the sauce and 5 minutes to reheat.

Preparation
Canned beets may also be used. Substitute canned juice for cooking liquid. Omit the 30-40 minutes cooking time and simply reheat in sauce.

Variation
Orange juice may be substituted for part of the vinegar measurement, if desired. Garnish with fresh orange slices for color.

SERVES 4

Stuffed Acorn Squash with a Rum Glaze

Squash has a subtle flavor that blends well with other ingredients.

2 even-sized acorn squash
⅓ cup butter or margarine
2 cooking apples, peeled, cored and cut into ½ inch pieces
½ cup pitted prunes, cut into large pieces
1 cup dried apricots, cut into large pieces
½ tsp ground allspice
6 tbsps rum
½ cup chopped walnuts
½ cup golden raisins
½ cup packed light brown sugar

1. Cut the squash in half lengthwise. Scoop out and discard the seeds.

2. Place the squash skin side up in a baking dish with water to come halfway up the sides. Bake for about 30 minutes at 350°F.

3. Melt half the butter in a saucepan and add the apple, prunes and apricots. Add the allspice and rum and bring to the boil. Lower the heat and simmer gently for about 5-10 minutes. Add the nuts and golden raisins 3 minutes before the end of cooking time.

4. Turn the squash over and fill the hollow with the fruit. Reserve the fruit cooking liquid.

5. Melt the remaining butter in a saucepan and stir in the brown sugar. Melt slowly until the sugar forms a syrup. Pour on fruit cooking liquid, stirring constantly. Bring back to the boil and cook until syrupy. Add more water if necessary.

6. Spoon the glaze onto each squash, over the fruit and the cut edge. Bake for a further 30 minutes, or until the squash is tender.

Step 2 Place the squash skin side up in a baking dish with water to pre-cook.

Step 5 Heat the butter and brown sugar in a saucepan until syrupy. Add the liquid from squash, stirring continuously.

Step 6 Spoon the glaze over each filled squash half, making sure to cover the cut edge.

Cook's Notes

Time
Preparation takes about 30 minutes and cooking takes about 1 hour.

Buying Guide
Acorn squash is a winter variety of squash and should have a very hard rind. The recipe may be prepared with other varieties of squash, such as butternut. These vegetables are available in large greengrocers and vegetable sections of larger supermarkets.

Serving Ideas
Serve as a side dish with turkey, chicken, ham or pork. If desired, add chopped cooked turkey, chicken or ham to the fruit filling and bake as directed. Serve as a light main course.

SERVES 6-8

Cranberry Orange Sauce

This North American berry, with its crisp taste and bright hue, is perfect with ham, chicken, pork and, of course, Thanksgiving turkey.

3 cups whole cranberries, fresh or frozen
Juice and rind of 2 large oranges
1 cup sugar

Step 2 Grate the oranges on the coarse side of a grater or use a zester to remove the rind.

1. Pick over the cranberries and remove any that are shrivelled or discolored.

2. Use the coarse side of the grater to grate the oranges. Take care not to remove too much of the white pith. Alternatively, remove the rind with a zester. Cut the oranges in half and squeeze them for juice.

3. Combine the sugar and orange rind in a deep saucepan and strain in the orange juice to remove the seeds. Bring to the boil and simmer for about 3 minutes, stirring continuously to dissolve the sugar.

4. When the sugar has dissolved, add the cranberries and cook until the skins pop, about 5 minutes. Remove from the heat and allow to cool slightly before serving. The sauce may also be served chilled.

Step 3 Combine the orange juice, rind and sugar in a deep saucepan, bring to the boil and cook until the sugar dissolves.

Step 4 Add the cranberries and cook until the skins pop.

Cook's Notes

Time
Preparation takes about 15 minutes, and cooking takes about 10 minutes.

Variations
Cranberry sauce may be prepared without the orange, simply substituting water for the orange juice. Alternatively, cook with red wine. Add cinnamon, cloves or allspice, if desired.

Preparation
Cranberry sauce may be prepared up to 1 week ahead of time and kept in the refrigerator, well covered.

SERVES 4

CREAMED ONIONS

Whole small onions in a creamy, rich sauce are part of Thanksgiving fare, but they are too good to save for just once a year.

1lb pearl onions
Boiling water to cover
2 cups milk
1 bay leaf
1 blade mace
2 tbsps butter or margarine
2 tbsps flour
Pinch salt and white pepper
Chopped parsley (optional)

Step 1 Trim down the root ends of each onion.

Step 2 Once the onions are boiled, put them into cold water and the peels should come off easily.

Step 3 Place the blade of mace and bay leaf in a saucepan with the milk, and heat until just beginning to boil.

1. Trim the root hairs on the onions but do not cut the roots off completely. Place the onions in a large saucepan and pour over the boiling water. Bring the onions back to the boil and cook for about 10 minutes.

2. Transfer the onions to cold water, allow to cool completely and then peel off the skins, removing roots as well. Leave the onions to drain dry.

3. Place the milk in a deep saucepan and add the blade mace and the bay leaf. Bring just to the boil, take off the heat and allow to stand for 15 minutes.

4. Melt the butter in a large saucepan and, when foaming, stir in the flour. Strain on the milk and discard the bay leaf and blade mace. Stir well and bring to the boil. Allow the sauce to simmer for about 3 minutes to thicken. Add salt and white pepper to taste and stir in the onions. Cook to heat through, but do not allow the sauce to boil again. Serve immediately and garnish with chopped parsley, if desired.

Cook's Notes

Time
Preparation takes about 30 minutes and cooking takes about 10 minutes for the onions and about 10 minutes for the sauce.

Preparation
Infusing the milk with the bay leaf and blade mace gives extra flavor to the sauce.

Cook's Tip
When adding onions to a white sauce, do not allow the sauce to boil as the onions can cause it to curdle.

SERVES 6

SUCCOTASH

A tasty side dish with a strange name, this was inherited from the American Indians, who made it a full meal by adding meat or poultry to it.

4 oz fresh or frozen corn
4 oz fresh or frozen lima beans
4 oz fresh or frozen green beans
3 tbsps butter
Salt and pepper
Chopped parsley

1. If using frozen vegetables, bring water to the boil in a saucepan and, when boiling, add the vegetables. Cook for about 5-8 minutes, drain and leave to dry.

2. If using fresh vegetables, bring water to the boil in a saucepan and add the lima beans first. After about 2 minutes, add the green beans. Follow these with the corn about 3 minutes before the end of cooking time. Drain and leave to dry.

3. Melt the butter in a saucepan and add the vegetables. Heat slowly, tossing or stirring occasionally, until heated through. Add salt and pepper to taste and stir in the parsley. Serve immediately.

Step 2 Cook all the vegetables in boiling water, adding them one after the other.

Step 3 Melt the butter in a saucepan and toss the vegetables over heat.

Cook's Notes

Time
Preparation takes about 10 minutes if using frozen vegetables and 25 minutes if using fresh vegetables. Cooking takes about 5-8 minutes for frozen vegetables and about 8-10 minutes for fresh vegetables.

Preparation
If using fresh vegetables, use a small, sharp knife to cut the kernels from the ears of the corn. Stand the corn on one end and cut down the length of the ear to separate the kernels. If using fresh lima beans, snap open the pods and push out the beans inside. If desired, the outer skin of the beans may be removed after cooking. Top and tail the fresh green beans and cut into 2 or 3 pieces.

Variation
Succotash can be made with just corn and lima beans or corn and green beans. Add red or green pepper, or chopped onion for flavor variation.

SERVES 4

POACHED CHICKEN WITH CREAM SAUCE

Plainly cooked chicken can be as flavorful as it is attractive.

4½lb whole roasting chicken
8-10 sticks celery, washed, cut into 3 inch lengths and tops reserved
4oz bacon, thickly sliced
2 cloves garlic, crushed
1 large onion, stuck with 4 cloves
1 bay leaf
1 sprig fresh thyme
Salt and pepper
Water to cover
⅓ cup butter or margarine
6 tbsps flour
1 cup light cream

---

1. Remove the fat from just inside the cavity of the chicken. Singe any pin feathers over gas flame or pull them out with tweezers.

2. Tie the chicken legs together and tuck the wing tips under to hold the neck flap. Place the chicken in a large casserole or stock pot. Chop the celery tops and add to the pot. Place the bacon over the chicken and add the garlic, onion with the cloves, bay leaf, sprig thyme, salt, pepper and water to cover.

3. Bring to the boil, reduce the heat and simmer gently, covered, for 50 minutes, or until the chicken is just tender.

4. Cut the celery into 3 inch lengths and add to the chicken. Simmer a further 20 minutes, or until the celery is just tender.

5. Remove the chicken to a serving plate and keep warm. Strain the stock and reserve the bacon and celery pieces. Skim fat off the top of the stock and add enough water to make up 2 cups, if necessary.

6. Melt 1 tbsp of the butter or margarine in the casserole and sauté the bacon until just crisp. Drain on paper towels and crumble roughly.

7. Melt the rest of the butter in the casserole or pan and when foaming take off the heat. Stir in the flour and gradually add the chicken stock. Add the cream and bring to the boil, stirring constantly. Simmer until the mixture is thickened.

8. Untie the legs and trim the leg ends. If desired, remove the skin from the chicken and coat with the sauce. Garnish with the bacon and the reserved celery pieces.

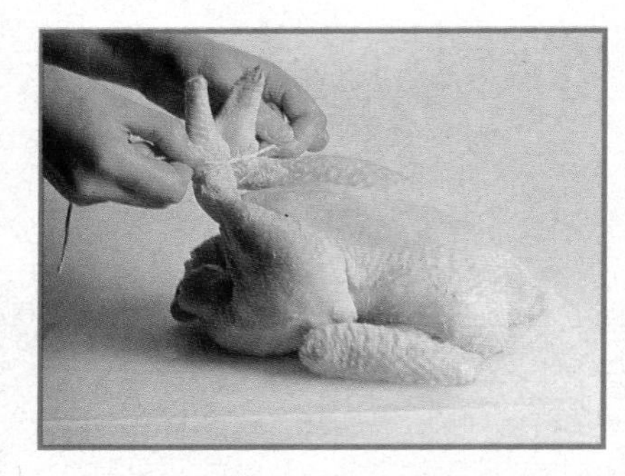

Step 2 Tie the legs together but do not cross them over. Tuck the neck skin under the wing tips.

Step 3 Arrange the bacon over the chicken, add the celery tops and the rest of the ingredients.

Cook's Notes

Time
Preparation takes about 25 minutes and cooking takes about 1 hour 10 minutes.

Serving Ideas
The chicken may be jointed into 8 pieces before coating with sauce, if desired. Cut the leg joints in two, dividing the thigh and the drumstick. Cut the breast in two, leaving some white meat attached to the wings. Cut through any bones with scissors.

Variation
Sliced or whole baby carrots may be added with the celery. Small onions may also be cooked with the celery and peeled in the same way as for the recipe for Creamed Onions.

SERVES 6

Chicken Pot Pie

Not a true pie, this dish is nevertheless warming winter fare with its creamy sauce and puffy biscuit topping.

4 chicken joints, 2 breasts and 2 legs
5 cups water
1 bay leaf
2 sprigs thyme
1 sprig rosemary
1 sprig fresh tarragon or 1/4 tsp dry tarragon
4 whole peppercorns
1 allspice berry
4 tbsps white wine
2 carrots, peeled and diced
24 pearl onions, peeled
6 tbsps frozen corn kernels
1/2 cup heavy cream
Salt

Biscuit Topping

3 1/2 cups all-purpose flour
1 1/2 tbsps baking powder
Pinch salt
5 tbsps butter or margarine
1 1/2 cups milk
1 egg, beaten with a pinch of salt

1. Place the chicken in a deep saucepan with water, herbs and spices and wine. Cover and bring to the boil. Reduce the heat and allow to simmer for 20-30 minutes, or until the chicken is tender. Remove the chicken from the pot and allow to cool. Skim and discard the fat from the surface of the stock. Skin the chicken and remove the meat from the bones.

2. Continue to simmer the stock until reduced by about half. Strain the stock and add the carrots and onions. Cook until tender and add the corn. Stir in the cream and add the chicken. Pour into a casserole or into individual baking dishes.

3. To prepare the topping, sift the dry ingredients into a bowl or place them in a food processor and process once or twice to sift.

4. Rub in the butter or margarine until the mixture resembles small peas. Stir in enough of the milk until the mixture comes together.

5. Turn out onto a floured surface and knead lightly. Roll out with a floured rolling pin and cut with a pastry cutter. Brush the surface of each biscuit with a mixture of egg and salt. Place the biscuits on top of the chicken mixture and bake for 10-15 minutes in a pre-heated oven at 375°F. Serve immediately.

Step 4 Rub the butter or margarine into the dry ingredients until the mixture resembles small peas.

Step 5 Roll out the biscuit mixture on a floured surface, cut into rounds and place on top of the chicken mixture.

Cook's Notes

Time
Preparation takes about 25 minutes and cooking takes about 20-30 minutes for the chicken, about 20 minutes to prepare the sauce, and about 10-15 minutes to finish off the dish.

Preparation
Once the biscuit topping has been prepared it must be baked immediately or the baking powder will stop working and the biscuits will not rise.

Variations
Diced potatoes and pimento may be added to the sauce along with other vegetables. Add chopped fresh parsley or a pinch of dried thyme as well, if desired.

SERVES 10-12

NEW ENGLAND ROAST TURKEY

The Thanksgiving celebration would not be the same without a turkey on the table. Native Indians first domesticated the bird and introduced the early settlers to it.

1 fresh turkey weighing about 20lbs
⅓ cup butter

Sausage Stuffing
4 tbsps oil
4oz sausage meat
3 sticks celery, diced
2 onions, diced
1 cup chopped walnuts or pecans
1 cup raisins
1lb day-old bread, made into small cubes
1 cup chicken stock
¼ tsp each dried thyme and sage
2 tbsps chopped fresh parsley
Salt and pepper

1. Singe any pin feathers on the turkey by holding the bird over a gas flame. Alternatively, pull out the feathers with tweezers.

2. Remove the fat which is just inside the cavity of the bird.

3. To prepare the stuffing, heat the oil and cook the sausage meat, breaking it up with a fork as it cooks. Add the celery, onion, nuts and raisins and cook for about 5 minutes, stirring constantly.

4. Drain away the fat and add the herbs, cubes of bread and stock, and mix well. Season to taste.

5. Stuff the cavity of the bird using your hands or a long-handled spoon. Save some stuffing to tuck under the neck flap to plump it.

6. Sew the cavity of the bird closed, or use skewers to secure it. Tie the legs together but do not cross them over. Tuck the neck skin under the wing tips and, if desired, use a trussing needle and fine string to secure them.

7. Place the turkey on a rack, breast side up, in a roasting pan. Soften the butter and spread some over the breast and the legs. Place the turkey in a pre-heated 325°F oven and cover loosely with foil. Roast for about 2 hours, basting often.

8. Remove the foil and continue roasting for another 2-2½ hours, or until the internal temperature in the thickest part of the thigh registers 350°F. Alternatively, pierce the thigh with a skewer – if the juices run clear then the turkey is done. Allow to rest for about 15-20 minutes before carving. Make gravy with the pan juices if desired and serve.

Step 8 Pierce the thigh with a skewer. The turkey is done when the juices run clear.

Cook's Notes

Variation
Many different ingredients can be included in a turkey stuffing. Ham or crisply cooked bacon can be substituted for the sausage. A mixture of dried fruit may be used instead of all raisins. Chopped apple may also be included.

Time
Preparation takes about 25-30 minutes and cooking takes about 4-4½hours.

Cook's Tip
Leaving a turkey or other roast bird to stand for 15-20 minutes before carving keeps the natural juices in the meat.

Watchpoint
The stuffing may be prepared in advance, but do not stuff the bird until ready to roast. There is a danger of food poisoning if a turkey or any other bird is stuffed too long before cooking.

SERVES 4

NEW ENGLAND BOILED DINNER

The "corning process" for preserving beef was a useful one in early America. The process took a long time, but fortunately we can now buy our beef already "corned"!

3lb corned beef brisket
1 bay leaf
1 tsp mustard seed
3 allspice berries
3 cloves
1 tsp dill seed
6 black peppercorns
2 potatoes, cut into even-sized pieces
4 small onions, peeled
4 large carrots, scraped
4 small or 2 large parsnips, peeled and cut into even-sized pieces
1 large or 2 small rutabagas
1 medium-size green cabbage, cored and quartered
Salt

1. Place the corned beef in a large saucepan with enough water to cover and add the bay leaf and spices. Cook for about 2 hours, skimming any foam from the surface as the meat cooks.

2. Add the potatoes and onions and cook for about 15 minutes. Taste and add salt if necessary.

3. Add the carrots, parsnips and rutabagas and cook for a further 15 minutes. Add the cabbage and cook a further 15 minutes.

4. Remove the meat from the casserole and slice it thinly. Arrange on a warm serving platter and remove the vegetables from the broth with a draining spoon, placing them around the meat. Serve immediately with horseradish or mustard.

Step 1 Combine the corned beef, salted water and spices in the pan. Bring to the boil, skimming the foam that rises to the surface.

Step 3 When the corned beef and root vegetables have cooked for 15 minutes, add the cabbage, pushing it under the liquid.

Step 4 Remove the meat from the pan and slice thinly across the grain.

Cook's Notes

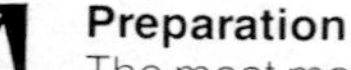

Preparation
The meat may be cooked for its first 2 hours in advance and refrigerated overnight if desired. Reheat and then add the vegetables according to the recipe.

Time
Preparation takes about 30 minutes and cooking takes about 3 hours.

Economy
Leftover corned beef is delicious for sandwiches, or for making corned beef hash.

Variation
Freshly-cooked beets may be added to the vegetable selection. Cook the beets separately or they will color all the vegetables and the meat. Substitute turnips for the rutabaga if desired.

SERVES 6-8

YANKEE POT ROAST

This classic American recipe has its roots in French and German cuisine. It is an excellent way with economical cuts of beef.

3lb beef roast (rump, chuck, round or top end)
Flour seasoned with salt and pepper
2 tbsps butter or margarine
1 onion stuck with 2 cloves
1 bay leaf
2 tsps fresh thyme or 1 tsp dried thyme
1 cup beef stock
4 carrots
12 small onions, peeled
4 small turnips, peeled and left whole
2 potatoes, cut into even-sized pieces
2 tbsps butter or margarine mixed with 2 tbsps flour

1. Dredge the beef with the seasoned flour, patting off the excess.

2. Melt the butter in a large, heavy-based casserole or saucepan and, when foaming, brown the meat on all sides, turning it with wooden spoons or a spatula.

3. When well browned, add the onion stuck with the cloves, bay leaf and thyme and pour on the stock. Cover the pan, reduce the heat and cook on top of the stove or in a pre-heated 300°F oven. Cook slowly for about 2 hours, adding more liquid, either stock or water, as necessary.

4. Test the meat and, if beginning to feel tender, add the vegetables. Cover and continue to cook until the meat is completely tender and the vegetables are cooked through.

5. Remove the meat and vegetables from the casserole or pan and place them on a warm serving platter. Skim the excess fat from the top of the sauce and bring it back to the boil.

6. Mix the butter and flour (beurre manie) to a smooth paste. Add about 1 tsp of the mixture to the boiling sauce and whisk thoroughly. Continue adding the mixture until the sauce is of the desired thickness. Carve the meat and spoon over some of the sauce. Serve the rest of the sauce separately.

Step 2 Place the meat in the hot fat to brown slowly and evenly. Use wooden spoons or a fish slice to turn.

Step 6 If the sauce needs thickening at the end, add a small spoonful of flour and butter paste and whisk well.

Cook's Notes

Time
Preparation takes about 30 minutes and cooking takes about 2-2½ hours.

Cook's Tip
The flour and butter paste or beurre manie may be prepared in large quantities and kept in the refrigerator or freezer to use any time thickening is necessary for a sauce.

Serving Ideas
This dish can be a meal in itself. If an accompaniment is desired, serve a green vegetable or a salad.

SERVES 4

RED FLANNEL HASH

The name comes from the color of the dish, made bright with the addition of cooked beets. It frequently features on brunch menus.

1lb cold corned beef
3-4 cold boiled potatoes, roughly chopped
1 medium onion, finely chopped
Salt, pepper and nutmeg
1-2 cooked beets, peeled and diced
2 tbsps butter or bacon fat

Step 1 Best results are obtained by chopping the meat into small dice by hand.

Step 2 Spread out the mixture in the hot fat in a frying pan.

Step 4 When a crust forms on the bottom, turn the mixture over to brown the other side.

1. Cut the meat into small pieces. If using a food processor, be careful not to overwork. Combine all the remaining ingredients except the butter or bacon fat.

2. Melt the butter or fat in a frying pan and, when foaming, place in the mixture. Spread it out evenly in the pan.

3. Cook over low heat, pressing the mixture down continuously with a wooden spoon or spatula. Cook about 15-20 minutes.

4. When a crust forms on the bottom, turn over and brown the other side. Cut into wedges and remove from the pan to serve.

Cook's Notes

Time
Preparation takes about 20 minutes if using leftover corned beef and potatoes from the New England Boiled Dinner recipe. Cooking takes about 25-30 minutes.

Serving Ideas
A freshly-poached egg may be placed on top of each serving of Red Flannel Hash. Serve with a mixture of mustard and horseradish, or horseradish and sour cream.

Economy
Use leftover corned beef from the New England Boiled Dinner or leftover roast beef for this recipe if desired.

SERVES 6-8

BOSTON BAKED BEANS

The first American "fast food", these beans were frozen and taken on long journeys to re-heat and eat en route.

1lb dried navy beans
5 cups water
4oz salt pork or slab bacon
1 onion, peeled and left whole
1 tsp dry mustard
1/3-1/2 cup molasses
Salt and pepper

Step 1 Soak the beans overnight so that they soften slightly and swell in size.

1. Soak the beans overnight in the water. Transfer to fresh water to cover. Bring to the boil and allow to cook for about 10 minutes. Drain and reserve the liquid.

2. Place the beans, salt pork or bacon and whole onion in a large, deep casserole or bean pot. Mix the molasses, mustard, salt and pepper with 1 cup of the reserved bean liquid. Stir into the beans and add enough bean liquid to cover. Expose only the pork rind on the salt pork and cover the casserole.

3. Bake in a pre-heated 300°F oven for about 2 hours. Add the remaining liquid, stirring well, and cook a further 1½ hours, or until the beans are tender. Uncover the beans for the last 30 minutes.

4. To serve, remove and discard the onion. Take out the salt pork or bacon and remove the rind. Slice or dice the meat and return to the beans. Check the seasoning and serve.

Step 2 Combine the beans, salt pork and onion with the molasses mixture.

Step 3 After the beans have baked for 2 hours, add remaining bean cooking liquid and stir well.

Cook's Notes

Time
Preparation takes about 20 minutes, with overnight soaking for the beans. Alternatively, bring the beans to the boil and then allow to stand for 2 hours. Cook as directed in the recipe. Total cooking takes about 3½ hours.

Preparation
The beans may be prepared well in advance and reheated just before serving. Leftovers may be frozen for up to 2 months.

Serving Ideas
Baked beans are traditionally served in Boston with steamed brown bread (see recipe). Sausages may be served with the beans, if desired.

SERVES 6-8

VENISON STEW

A recipe very similar to the country stews of France, this one made use of the abundant game found in the New England colonies.

3lbs venison shoulder or leg, cut into 2 inch pieces
2 cups dry red wine
4 tbsps red wine vinegar
1 bay leaf
2 tsps chopped fresh thyme or 1 tsp dried thyme
6 juniper berries, crushed
3 whole allspice berries
6 black peppercorns
1 clove garlic, crushed
4 tbsps oil
2 carrots, cut into strips
1 onion, thinly sliced
2 sticks celery, cut into strips
8oz mushrooms, sliced
Chopped parsley to garnish

1. Combine the wine, vinegar, bay leaf, thyme, juniper berries, allspice, peppercorns and garlic with the venison, and marinate overnight.

2. Remove the meat from the marinade and pat dry on paper towels. Reserve the marinade for later use.

3. Heat the oil in a heavy frying pan or casserole and brown the venison on all sides over very high heat. Brown in several small batches if necessary. Remove the venison and lower the heat. If using a frying pan, transfer the venison to an ovenproof casserole.

4. Lower the heat and brown the vegetables in the oil until golden. Sprinkle over the flour and cook until the flour browns lightly. Combine the vegetables with the venison and add the reserved marinade.

5. Cover and cook the stew in a pre-heated 300°F oven for about 2 hours.

6. Fifteen minutes before the end of cooking time, add the mushrooms and continue cooking until the meat is tender. Garnish with parsley before serving.

Step 1 Combine the venison, wine, vinegar, herbs and spices in a polythene bag and tie securely. Place in a bowl to catch any drips and turn the bag often to marinate evenly.

Step 4 When the vegetables and flour have browned, combine them with the browned meat. Gradually pour marinade over the ingredients, stirring well.

Cook's Notes

Time
Preparation takes about 30 minutes, plus overnight marinating. Cooking takes about 10 minutes for the meat to brown and about 2 hours for the stew to cook.

Preparation
The stew may be prepared in advance and refrigerated, which will intensify the flavour. Reheat slowly, but bring briefly to the boil before serving.

Serving Ideas
Serve with chestnut purée, mashed potatoes or boiled potatoes. Add a green vegetable or salad if desired.

SERVES 4

BOSTON SCROD

Scrod, or baby codfish, provides the perfect base for a crunchy, slightly spicy topping. Boston is justly famous for it.

4 even-sized cod fillets
Salt and pepper
1/3 cup butter, melted
3/4 cup dry breadcrumbs
1 tsp dry mustard
1 tsp onion salt
Dash Worcester sauce and tabasco
2 tbsps lemon juice
1 tbsp finely chopped parsley

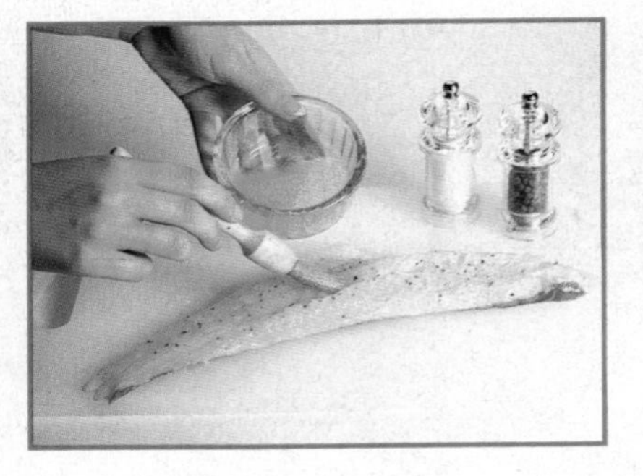

Step 1 Season the fish lightly with salt and pepper and brush with some of the melted butter. Broil to pre-cook but do not brown.

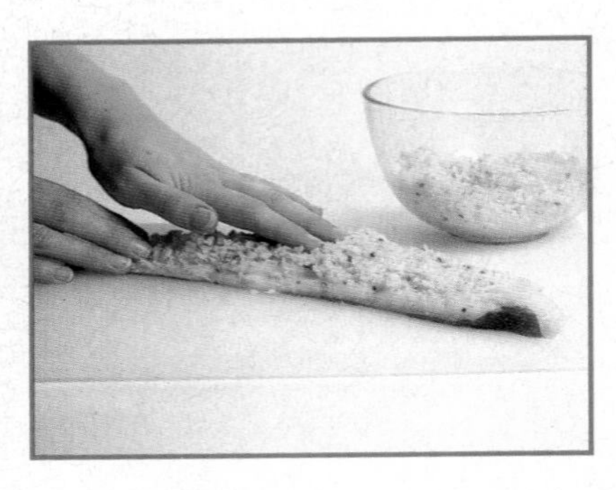

Step 3 Press the crumbs gently to pack them into place using a spoon or your hand.

1. Season the fish fillets with salt and pepper and place them on a broiler tray. Brush with butter and broil for about 5 minutes.

2. Combine remaining butter with breadcrumbs, mustard, onion salt, Worcester sauce, tabasco, lemon juice and parsley.

3. Spoon the mixture carefully on top of each fish fillet, covering it completely. Press down lightly to pack the crumbs into place. Broil for a further 5-7 minutes, or until the top is lightly browned and the fish flakes.

Cook's Notes

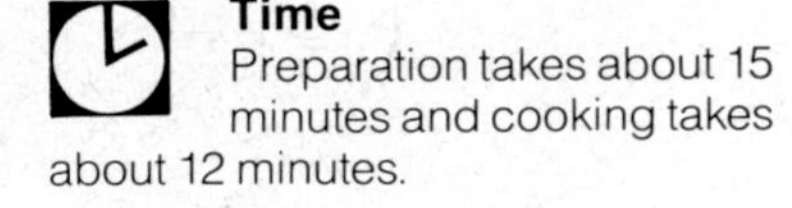

Time
Preparation takes about 15 minutes and cooking takes about 12 minutes.

Preparation
If desired, the fish may also be baked in the oven Cover the fish with foil for first 5 minutes ot baking time, uncover and top with the breadcrumb mixture. Bake for a further 10-12 minutes at 350°F.

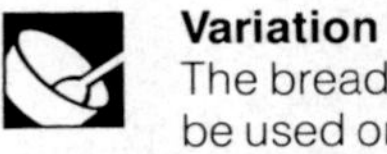

Variation
The breadcrumb topping may be used on other fish such as haddock, halibut or sole.

SERVES 4

NEW ENGLAND BOUILLABAISSE

French settlers brought this favorite recipe to the New World, and just as they would have at home, they used local, seasonal ingredients in it.

Stock

1lb fish bones, skin and heads
7 cups water
1 small onion, thinly sliced
1 small carrot, thinly sliced
1 bay leaf
6 black peppercorns
1 blade mace
1 sprig thyme
2 lemon slices

Bouillabaisse

⅓ cup butter or margarine
1 carrot, sliced
3 leeks, well washed and thinly sliced
1 clove garlic
Pinch saffron
⅓-½ cup dry white wine
8oz canned tomatoes
1 lobster
1lb cod or halibut fillets
1lb mussels, well scrubbed
1 lb small clams, well scrubbed
8 new potatoes, scrubbed but not peeled
Chopped parsley
8oz large shrimp, peeled and de-veined

1. First prepare the fish stock. Place all the ingredients in a large stock pot and bring to the boil over high heat. Lower the heat and allow to simmer for 20 minutes. Strain and reserve the stock. Discard the fish bones and vegetables.

2. Melt the butter in a medium-sized saucepan and add the carrots, leeks and garlic. Cook for about 5 minutes until slightly softened.

3. Add the saffron and wine and allow to simmer for about 5 minutes.

4. Add the fish stock along with all the remaining bouillabaise ingredients except the shrimp. Bring the mixture to the boil and cook until the lobster turns red, the mussel and clam shells open and the potatoes are tender. Turn off the heat and add the shrimp. Cover the pan and let the shrimp cook in the residual heat. Divide the ingredients among 4 soup bowls. Remove the lobster and cut it in half. Divide the tail between the other 2 bowls and serve the bouillabaisse with garlic bread.

Step 2 Cook the carrots, leeks and garlic in butter until soft but not colored. Combine all the bouillabaisse ingredients in a large stock pot.

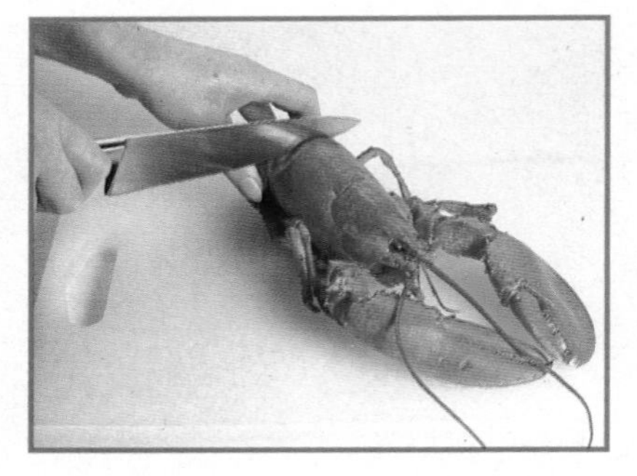

Step 4 Remove the lobster and cut it in half using a large, sharp knife.

Cook's Notes

Time
Preparation takes about 35 minutes and cooking takes about 30 minutes.

Watchpoint
Leeks must be split in half first and rinsed under cold water to remove sand and grit before slicing.

Variation
Use whatever shellfish or fish is in season or suits your taste. Lobster is not essential.

SERVES 4

Whole Baked Fish with New England Stuffing

A whole fish, perfectly cooked, never fails to impress. With a stuffing of oysters, it is certainly grand enough for an important dinner party.

4¼lb whole fish, gutted and boned (use salmon, salmon trout or sea bass)

Stuffing

8oz savory cracker crumbs
¼ cup butter, melted
Pinch salt and pepper
2 tsps lemon juice
¼ tsp each dried thyme, sage and marjoram
1 shallot, finely chopped
10 oysters, shelled

Step 2 Place the prepared fish on lightly-greased foil, shiny side up.

Step 3 Spoon the stuffing into the cavity of the fish.

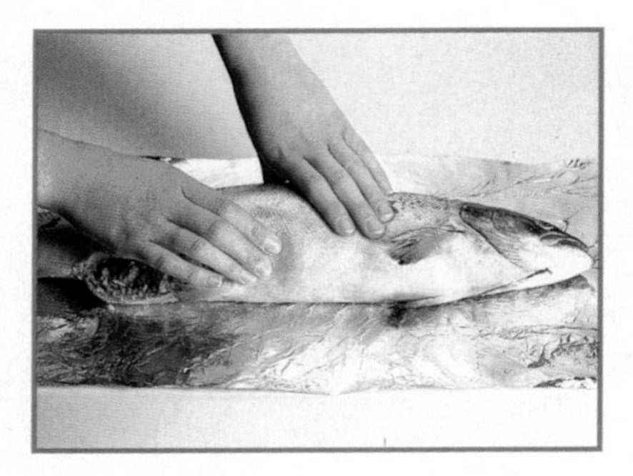

Step 4 Pat the fish to distribute the stuffing evenly.

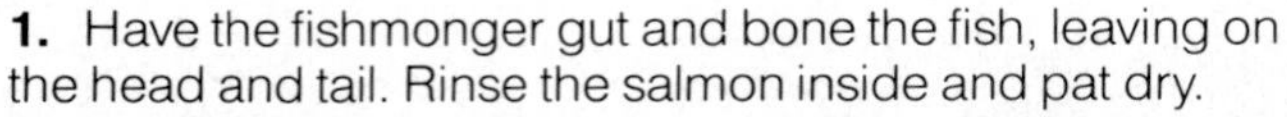

1. Have the fishmonger gut and bone the fish, leaving on the head and tail. Rinse the salmon inside and pat dry.
2. Place the fish on lightly oiled foil. Combine all the stuffing ingredients, mixing so that the oysters do not fall apart.
3. Open the cavity of the fish and spoon in the stuffing.
4. Close the fish and pat out gently so that the stuffing is evenly distributed. Close the foil loosely around the fish and place it directly on the oven shelf or in a large roasting pan. Cook at 400°F for about 40 minutes. Unwrap the fish and slide it onto a serving plate. Peel off the top layer of skin if desired and garnish with lemon slices.

Time
Preparation takes about 25 minutes and cooking takes about 40 minutes.

Preparation
If asked, the fishmonger will gut and bone the fish for you. Fish may also be stuffed with the bone in, but this makes it more difficult to serve.

Variation
Substitute mussels, clams or shrimp for the oysters in the stuffing. Add chopped celery or red or green pepper, if desired.

SERVES 4-6

BOATMAN'S STEW

This quick, economical and satisfying fish dish will please any fish lover for lunch or a light supper.

6 tbsps olive oil
2 large onions, sliced
1 red pepper, seeded and sliced
4oz mushrooms, sliced
1lb canned tomatoes
Pinch salt and pepper
Pinch dried thyme
1½ cups water
2lb whitefish fillets, skinned
½ cup white wine
2 tbsps chopped parsley

Use a sharp knife to cut the onion into thin crosswise slices.

1. Heat the oil in a large saucepan and add the onions. Cook until beginning to look transluscent. Add the pepper and cook until the vegetables are softened.

2. Add the mushrooms and the tomatoes and bring the mixture to the boil.

3. Add thyme, salt, pepper and water and simmer for about 30 minutes.

4. Add the fish and wine and cook until the fish flakes easily, about 15 minutes. Stir in parsley.

5. To serve, place a piece of toasted French bread in the bottom of the soup bowl and spoon over the fish stew.

Step 1 Cook the onions in the oil along with the peppers until soft.

Cook's Notes

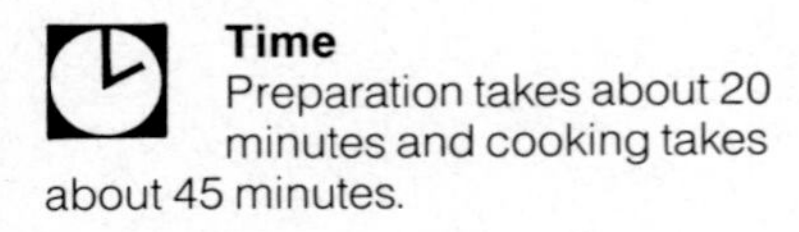

Time
Preparation takes about 20 minutes and cooking takes about 45 minutes.

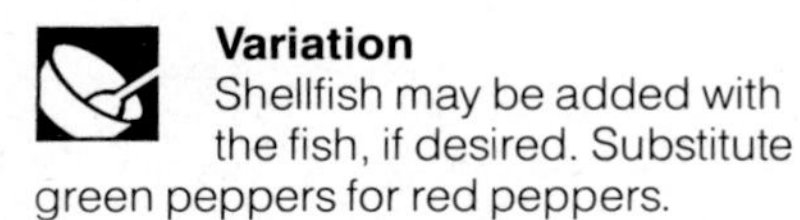

Variation
Shellfish may be added with the fish, if desired. Substitute green peppers for red peppers.

Serving Ideas
The stew may also be served over rice. Accompany with a green salad.

SERVES 4

Boiled Maine Lobster

With today's lobster prices, it's hard to imagine that American colonists considered this delectable seafood humble and ordinary.

4 1lb lobsters
Water
Salt or seaweed
1 cup melted butter
Lemon wedges
Parsley sprigs

Step 5 Once the claws are removed from the lobster by twisting off, crack each claw with a nutcracker, hammer or special lobster cracking tool.

1. Fill a large stock pot full of water and add salt or a piece of seaweed. Bring the water to the boil and then turn off the heat.

2. Place the live lobsters into the pot, keeping your hand well away from the claws. Lower them in claws first.

3. Bring the water slowly back to the boil and cook the lobsters for about 15 minutes, or until they turn bright red.

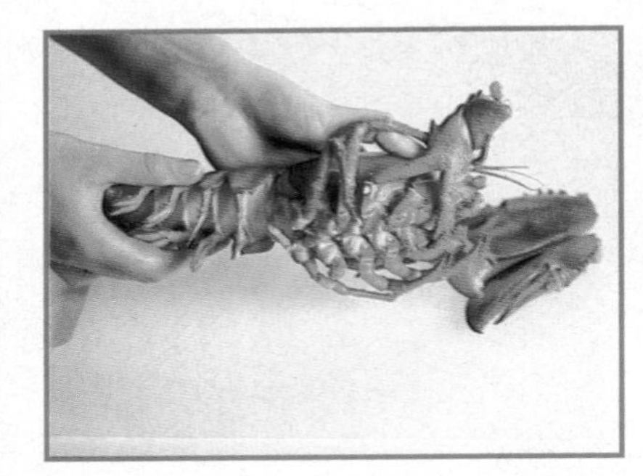

Step 6 Separate body from tail by arching the lobster backwards. Break off the flipper and push the tail meat out with a fork.

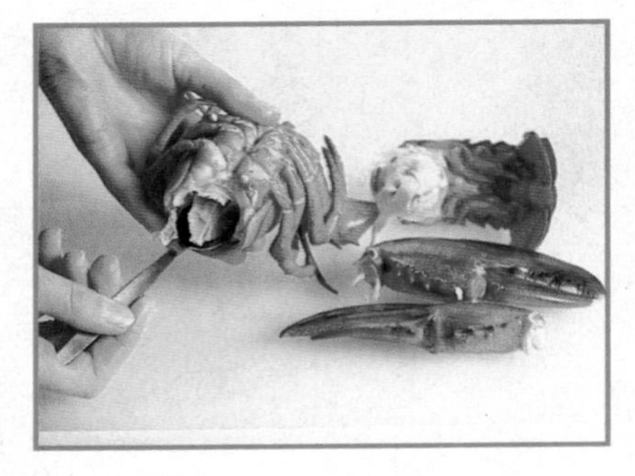

Step 7 Remove the back from the body and discard the stomach sac and lungs. Retain the tomalley or liver to eat, if desired, and crack open the body to extract any remaining meat.

4. Remove them from the water and drain briefly on paper towels. Place on a plate and garnish the plate with lemon wedges and parsley sprigs. Serve with individual dishes of melted butter for dipping.

Cook's Notes

Time
Allow about 20 minutes for the water to boil, and 15 minutes for cooking the lobster.

Preparation
This method of cooking puts the lobster gently to sleep and makes the lobster flesh much more tender. Claws can be partially cracked before serving, if desired.

Cook's Tip
Lobster may be cooked in this way for a variety of recipes that are based on pre-cooked lobster.

SERVES 4-6

MAPLE SYRUP MOUSSE

Pure maple syrup is a true delicacy. It isn't cheap, but the flavor it gives special recipes like this mousse makes it worth its price.

4 eggs, separated
2 extra egg whites
¾ cup maple syrup
1 cup heavy cream
Chopped pecans or walnuts to decorate

1. Place the syrup in a saucepan and bring to the boil. Continue boiling to reduce the syrup by one quarter.
2. Beat the egg yolks until thick and lemon colored.
3. Pour the maple syrup onto the egg yolks in a thin, steady stream, beating with an electric mixer. Continue beating until the mixture has cooled.
4. Beat the egg whites until stiff but not dry and whip the cream until soft peaks form.
5. Fold the cream and egg whites into the maple mixture and spoon into a serving bowl or individual glasses. Refrigerate until slightly set and top with chopped walnuts or pecans to serve.

Step 3 Pour the hot syrup onto the beaten egg yolks in a thin, steady stream, beating constantly.

Step 5 Fold the cream and the egg whites into the maple mixture using a rubber spatula or large metal spoon.

Cook's Notes

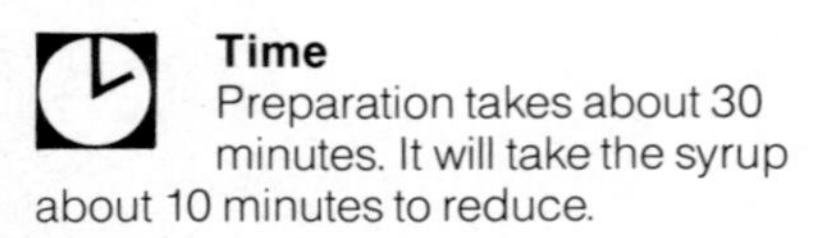

Time
Preparation takes about 30 minutes. It will take the syrup about 10 minutes to reduce.

Variation
Finely chopped pieces of maple sugar can be used instead of nuts to decorate the top of the mousse.

Watchpoint
Be careful when boiling the syrup, since it can burn very easily.

MAKES 1 PIE

PUMPKIN PIE

American Indians taught the settlers about the pumpkin and it was one of the crops that helped to save their lives.

Pastry
1 cup all-purpose flour
Pinch salt
¼ cup butter, margarine or lard
Cold milk

Pumpkin Filling
1lb cooked and mashed pumpkin
2 eggs
1 cup evaporated milk
½ cup brown sugar
1 tsp ground cinnamon
¼ tsp ground allspice
Pinch nutmeg
Pecan halves for decoration

Step 1 Rub the fat into the flour until the mixture resembles fine breadcrumbs.

1. To prepare the pastry, sift the flour and a pinch of salt into a mixing bowl. Rub in the fat until the mixture resembles fine breadcrumbs. Stir in enough cold milk to bring the mixture together into a firm ball. Cover and chill for about 30 minutes before use.

2. Roll out the pastry on a lightly-floured surface to a circle about 11 inches in diameter.

Step 1 Add enough cold milk to bring the mixture together into a firm ball.

Step 3 Roll the pastry around a lightly-floured rolling pin and then lower it into the dish.

3. Wrap the pastry around a lightly-floured rolling pin and lower it into a 10 inch round pie dish.

4. Press the pastry into the dish and flute the edge or crimp with a fork.

5. Prick the base lightly with the tines of a fork.

6. Combine all the filling ingredients in a mixing bowl and beat with an electric mixer until smooth. Alternatively, use a food processor. Pour into the pie crust and bake in a pre-heated 425°F oven. Bake for 10 minutes at this temperature and then lower the temperature to 350°F and bake for a further 40-50 minutes, or until the filling is set. Decorate with a circle of pecan halves.

Cook's Notes

Time
Preparation takes about 30 minutes and cooking takes about 50-60 minutes.

Cook's Tip
Pricking the base of the pastry lightly will prevent it from rising up in an air bubble in the middle of the pie.

Serving Ideas
Serve warm or cold with whipped cream.

MAKES 1 PIE

BLUEBERRY PIE

Americans love pie for dessert. In New England, where blueberries flourish, it's only natural to find them in a pie.

Double quantity pastry for Pumpkin Pie recipe

Filling

1lb blueberries
2 tbsps cornstarch
4 tbsps water
2 tbsps lemon juice
1 cup sugar
1 egg beaten with a pinch of salt

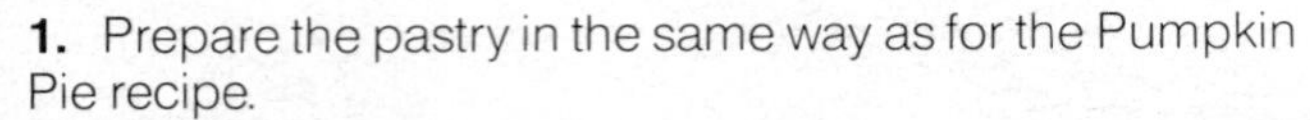

1. Prepare the pastry in the same way as for the Pumpkin Pie recipe.

2. Divide the pastry in half and roll out one half to form the base. Use a floured rolling pin to lower it into the dish, and press it against the sides. Chill the pastry in the dish and the remaining half of the pastry while preparing the filling.

3. Place the fruit in a bowl and mix the cornstarch with the water and lemon juice. Pour it over the fruit, add the sugar and mix together gently.

4. Spoon the fruit filling into the pastry base.

5. Roll out the remaining pastry on a lightly-floured surface and cut it into strips.

6. Use the strips to make a lattice pattern on top of the filling and press the edges to stick them to the pastry base. Cut off any excess pastry.

7. Using your fingers or a fork, crimp the edges to decorate.

8. Brush the crimped edge of the pastry and the lattice strips lightly with the beaten egg and bake in a pre-heated 425°F oven for about 10 minutes. Reduce the heat to 350°F and bake for a further 40-45 minutes. Serve warm or cold.

Step 4 Spoon the blueberry filling into the pastry-lined pie dish.

Step 6 Cut strips of pastry and use to make a lattice pattern on top of the pie.

Step 7 Crimp by hand, or use a fork to make a decorative edge.

Time
Preparation takes about 30-40 minutes and cooking takes about 50-55 minutes.

Cook's Tip
Taste the blueberries before deciding how much sugar to add – it may not be necessary to add the full amount.

Variation
Other fruits such as raspberries or blackberries may be used in the pie instead of blueberries.

Steamed Cranberry Pudding

Colonial women brought their favorite recipes with them and learned to adapt them to the local produce, hence an English steamed pudding with American cranberries.

1½ cups all-purpose flour
2 tsps baking powder
Pinch salt
1 cup chopped cranberries
1 small piece candied ginger, finely chopped
2 eggs, well beaten
½ cup honey
6 tbsps milk
Orange sauce
Grated juice and rind of 1 orange
Grated juice and rind of ½ lemon
½ cup sugar
1 tbsp cornstarch
¾ cup water
1 tbsp butter or margarine

1. Sift the dry ingredients together in a large bowl.

2. Toss in the cranberries and ginger.

3. Mix the eggs, honey and milk together and gradually stir into the dry ingredients and the cranberries. Do not over stir. The mixture should not be uniformly pink.

4. The mixture should be of thick dropping consistency. Add more milk if necessary.

5. Spoon the mixture into a well-buttered pudding basin or bowl, cover with buttered foil and tie the top securely.

6. Place the bowl on a rack in a pan of boiling water to come halfway up the sides. Cover the pan and steam the pudding for about 1½ hours, or until a skewer inserted into the center comes out clean. Leave to cool in the basin or bowl for about 10 minutes, loosen the edge with a knife and turn out onto a plate.

7. Meanwhile, place the sugar and cornstarch into a saucepan with the orange juice and rind and lemon juice and rind. Add the water, stirring to blend well. Bring to the boil and allow to simmer until clear. Beat in the butter at the end and serve with the pudding.

Step 3 Stir the liquid ingredients into the dry until well blended and of thick dropping consistency.

Step 5 Spoon into the prepared bowl or basin. Cover the top with foil and tie securely with string.

Cook's Notes

Time
Preparation takes about 30-40 minutes and cooking takes about 1½ hours.

Buying Guide
Fresh cranberries are available in greengrocers and larger supermarkets. Frozen cranberries are also available and may be substituted for fresh.

Variation
If desired, use ground ginger instead of the candied ginger.

Orange Bread Pudding

Bread puddings came to America from England and they remain as popular as ever in both countries.

4 cups milk
8 slices white bread, crusts removed
4 tbsps butter or margarine
6 egg yolks
3 egg whites
1 tbsp orange flower water
¾ cup sugar
½ tsp freshly ground nutmeg
Pinch salt
½ cup orange marmalade

1. Heat the milk until just scalded.

2. In a large bowl, break the bread into cubes and add the butter. Stir in the hot milk until the butter is melted and the bread has broken up. Allow the mixture to cool to luke-warm.

3. Lightly grease a large soufflé dish or pudding basin.

4. Combine the egg yolks and whites with the orange flower water in a bowl, and beat until frothy. Stir in the sugar, nutmeg and salt. Stir the egg mixture into the bread and milk mixture until just combined, and pour into the prepared mold.

5. Cover the mold with lightly greased foil and tie tightly. Place the dish on a rack in a large saucepan and fill with boiling water to within 1 inch of the top of the bowl.

6. Bring the water to boiling and then allow to simmer, covered, for 1½ hours, or until the pudding is firm in the center.

7. Allow to cool for about 30 minutes and then loosen the edge with a knife. Invert onto a serving plate to unmold.

8. Spread the top with orange marmalade and serve warm or cold.

Step 4 Pour the pudding mixture into a lightly-greased mold. Pour to within about 1 inch of the top of the mold.

Step 7 When the pudding has cooled slightly, loosen the edge with a knife.

Step 8 Place a plate on top and then turn the pudding over to unmold.

Cook's Notes

Time
Preparation takes about 30 minutes and cooking takes about 1½ hours.

Cook's Tip
If serving the pudding cold, loosen the edge and then allow it to cool completely in the mold before unmolding. This makes turning the pudding out a lot easier.

Watchpoint
Carefully check the level of water in the kettle at intervals. Do not allow the pudding to boil dry.

MAKES 1 LOAF

Spiced Cranberry Nut Bread

Sassamanesh was the colorful Indian name for this equally colorful berry. Here, it brightens up a quickly prepared bread.

2 cups all-purpose flour
1 tsp baking powder
1 cup sugar
1 tsp baking soda
Pinch salt
¼ tsp ground nutmeg
¼ tsp ground ginger
½ cup orange juice
2 tbsps butter or margarine, melted
4 tbsps water
1 egg
1 cup fresh cranberries, roughly chopped
1 cup hazelnuts, roughly chopped

Step 1 Sift the dry ingredients into a bowl and make a well in the center.

1. Sift the dry ingredients and spices into a large mixing bowl. Make a well in the center of the dry ingredients and pour in the orange juice, melted butter or margarine, water and egg. Using a wooden spoon, beat the liquid mixture, gradually drawing in the flour from the outside edge.

2. Add the cranberries and nuts and stir to mix completely.

3. Lightly grease a loaf pan about 9 x 5″. Press a strip of wax paper on the base and up the sides. Lightly grease the paper and flour the whole inside of the pan. Spoon or pour in the bread mixture and bake in a pre-heated 325°F oven for about 1 hour, or until a skewer inserted into the center of the loaf comes out clean.

4. Remove from the pan, carefully peel off the paper and cool on a wire rack. Lightly dust with confectioner's sugar, if desired, and cut into slices to serve.

Step 1 Pour the liquid ingredients into the well and, using a wooden spoon, stir to gradually incorporate the flour from the outside edge.

Step 2 Fold in the cranberries and the nuts.

Cook's Notes

Time
Preparation takes about 25 minutes and cooking takes about 1 hour.

Watchpoint
Be sure to bake the bread mixture as soon as possible after the baking powder has been added or the bread will not rise the way it should.

Serving Ideas
Serve warm with butter or cream cheese with tea or coffee. May also be served cold.

STEAMED BROWN BREAD

This is the classic accompaniment to one of Boston's famous dishes – baked beans. It's traditional to bake it in a can!

1½ cups fine cornmeal
2 cups wholewheat flour
1 cup all-purpose flour
Pinch salt
⅓ cup molasses mixed with 1 tsp bicarbonate of soda
1½ cups cold water
Butter or oil
Boiling water

Step 3 Grease rinsed out cans generously with butter or margarine.

Step 3 Fill the cans with the bread mixture to about two thirds full.

Step 4 Cover the tops of the cans tightly with foil and place on a rack in boiling water to come halfway up the sides.

1. Sift the dry ingredients into a large bowl and return the bran to the bowl.

2. Mix the molasses, bicarbonate of soda and water together. Make a well in the center of the flour and pour in the mixture. Mix just until well blended.

3. Use a large can from canned tomatoes, coffee or canned fruit. Alternatively, use about 6 smaller cans. Wash them well and remove the labels. Grease generously with oil or butter. Spoon the bread mixture to come about two thirds of the way up the sides of the cans.

4. Cover the tops of the cans tightly with buttered or oiled foil. Place them on a rack in a deep saucepan. Pour enough boiling water around the cans to come about halfway up the sides. Allow water to bubble gently to steam the bread for 3-4 hours in the covered pan. Add more boiling water as necessary during cooking.

5. The bread is ready when a skewer inserted into the center of the bread comes out clean.

Time
Preparation takes about 20 minutes and cooking takes about 3-4 hours. Cooking time may be slightly shorter for smaller cans.

Variation
Raisins, chopped dates or prunes may be added to the bread mixture if desired.

Serving Ideas
This bread is the traditional accompaniment to Boston Baked Beans. Alternatively, serve warm with butter or cream cheese.

INDEX

Compiled by Judith Ferguson
Photographed by Peter Barry
Recipes Prepared for Photography by
Bridgeen Deery and Wendy Devenish